Thomas Kinsella
A Dublin Documentary

THOMAS KINSELLA was born in Dublin in 1928. He attended University College, Dublin, and entered the Irish Civil Service in 1946. He left the Department of Finance in 1965 to become writer in residence at the University of Southern Illinois, later becoming professor of English at Temple University, Philadelphia. Early titles include *Another September* (1958), *Downstream* (1962) and *Nightwalker and Other Poems* (1968) – all choices of the Poetry Book Society. Other publications include *Notes from the Land of the Dead* (1972), *Fifteen Dead* (1976) and *Song of the Night* (1978). Translations from the Irish include *The Táin* (1969) and *An Duanaire: Poems of the Dispossessed, 1600–1900* (1980). A director of Dolmen Press and Cuala Press, Kinsella also founded his own imprint, Peppercanister, in 1972, to publish pamphlets of poetry.

Early awards included the Guinness Poetry Award in 1958 and the Irish Arts Council Triennial Book Award in 1960. He received the Denis Devlin Memorial Award in 1966, 1969, 1988 and 1994, and was awarded Guggenheim Fellowships in 1968/9 and 1971/2.

He was editor of the *New Oxford Book of Irish Verse* (1986) and published a critical view, *The Dual Tradition: An Essay on Poetry and Politics in Ireland*, in 1995. His *Collected Poems* was published by Carcanet in 2001. *Marginal Economy*, a collection of poems, and *Readings in Poetry*, introducing a series of close readings of notable poems, were both published in 2006.

Thomas Kinsella

A Dublin Documentary

THE O'BRIEN PRESS
DUBLIN

First published 2006 by The O'Brien Press Ltd,
12 Terenure Road East, Rathgar, Dublin 6, Ireland.
Tel: +353 1 4923333; Fax: +353 1 4922777
E-mail: books@obrien.ie
Website: www.obrien.ie

ISBN-10: 0-86278-995-8
ISBN-13: 978-0-86278-995-4

British Library Cataloguing-in-Publication Data
Kinsella, Thomas
A Dublin Documentary
1. Dublin (Ireland) - Poetry
I. Title
821.9'14

1 2 3 4 5 6 7 8 9 10
06 07 08 09 10 11

Editing, typesetting, layout and design: The O'Brien Press Ltd
Printing: MPG Books

CONTENTS

part I:
... imaginative beginnings ...

I am not, technically a Dubliner, despite being born and reared in Inchicore. I am told that for the full qualification three generations born in the city are needed. My children would qualify, if they wished; my parents were born in Dublin.

Their own parents were all born in the country. My mother's parents, the Casserlys, came from Ballinafid in County Westmeath; the Kinsellas from Tinahely in County Wicklow. Grandfather Casserly, 'the Boss', was employed by an insurance company as a collector; he was a man about town, unreliable on his bicycle. Grandfather Kinsella was a quieter person, long retired from Guinness's when I knew him: deaf and gentle and bald, a repairer of shoes.

The wives of these men were formidable women. They both managed small shops in their houses: one in Basin Lane, off James's Street, near the Canal, not far from the Brewery; the other in Bow Lane, on the other side of James's Street, close to the end wall of Swift's hospital, and at the start of the road leading toward Kilmainham, out of Dublin.

It was in a world dominated by these people that I remember many things of importance happening to me for the first time. And it is in their world that I came to terms with these things as best I could, and later set my attempts at understanding.

In the Casserly home, in a room behind the shop, the family would gather at week-ends, playing cards. Some of my first awarenesses are placed in the dark of that room, taking in the textures of life in their random detail: the firelight on the shelves of the dresser and on the card table; the voices of the players familiar and mysterious:

A Hand of Solo

Lips and tongue
wrestle the delicious
      life out of you.

A last drop.
Wonderful.
      A moment's rest.

In the firelight glow
the flickering
      shadows softly

come and go up on the shelf:
red heart and black spade
      hid in the kitchen dark.

Woman throat song
help my head
      back to you sweet.

      *

Hushed, buried green baize.
Slide and stop. Black spades. Tray. Still.
Red deuce. Two hearts. Blood-clean. Still.

Black flash. Jack Rat grins.
She drops down. Silent. Face disk blank. Queen.

The Boss spat in the kitchen fire.
His head shook.

Angus's fat hand brushed in all the pennies.
His waistcoat pressed the table.

Uncle Matty slithered the cards together
and knocked them. Their edges melted. Soft gold.

Angus picked up a bright penny and put it
in my hand: satiny, dream-new disk of light...

'Go on out in the shop and get yourself something.'
'Now Angus...'

                  'Now, now, Jack. He's my luck.'
'Tell your grandmother we're waiting for her.'

She was settling the lamp.
Two yellow tongues rose and brightened.
The shop brightened.

Her eyes glittered.
A tin ghost beamed, Mick McQuaid
nailed across the fireplace.

'Shut the kitchen door, child of grace.
Come here to me.
Come here to your old grandmother.'

Strings of jet beads wreathed her neck
and hissed on the black taffeta
and crept on my hair.

My eyes were squeezed shut against the key
in the pocket of her apron. Her stale abyss...
'...You'd think I had three heads!'

Old knuckles pressed on the counter,
then were snatched away. She sat down at the till
on her high stool, chewing nothing.

The box of Indian apples
was over in the corner
by the can of oil.

I picked out one of the fruit,
a rose-red hard wax
turning toward gold, light like wood,

and went at it with little bites,
peeling off bits of skin
and tasting the first traces of the blood.

When it was half peeled,
with the glassy pulp exposed like cells,
I sank my teeth in it

loosening the packed mass of dryish beads
from their indigo darkness.
I drove my tongue among them

and took a mouthful, and slowly
bolted them. My throat filled
with a rank, Arab bloodstain.

Indian apple was our name for the pomegranate. There was a strangeness about it. And about many things: the two rooms at the end of a dark passageway, where the grandparents spent a lot of their time, and seemed very dark in themselves.

Also the yard outside, a silent square courtyard at the back, off Basin Lane, with a couple of whitewashed cottages in the corners, with half-doors. A separate world, with a few other people, and cats and hens and a feel of the country. A whole place that has long disappeared.

Hen Woman

The noon heat in the yard
smelled of stillness and coming thunder.
A hen scratched and picked at the shore.
It stopped, its body crouched and puffed out.
The brooding silence seemed to say 'Hush...'

The cottage door opened,
a black hole
in a whitewashed wall so bright
the eyes narrowed.
Inside, a clock murmured 'Gong...'

(I had felt all this before.)

She hurried out in her slippers
muttering, her face dark with anger,
and gathered the hen up jerking
languidly. Her hand fumbled.
Too late. Too late.

It fixed me with its pebble eyes
(seeing what mad blur).
A white egg showed in the sphincter;
mouth and beak opened together;
and time stood still.

Nothing moved: bird or woman,
fumbled or fumbling – locked there
(as I must have been) gaping.

                    *

There was a tiny movement at my feet,
tiny and mechanical; I looked down.
A beetle like a bronze leaf
was inching across the cement,
clasping with small tarsi
a ball of dung bigger than its body.

The serrated brow pressed the ground humbly,
lifted in a short stare, bowed again;
the dung-ball advanced minutely,
losing a few fragments,
specks of staleness and freshness.

$$*$$

A mutter of thunder far off
– time not quite stopped.
I saw the egg had moved a fraction:
a tender blank brain
under torsion, a clean new world.

As I watched, the mystery completed.
The black zero of the orifice
closed to a point
and the white zero of the egg hung free,
flecked with greenish brown oils.

It fell and turned over slowly.
Dreamlike, fussed by her splayed fingers,
it floated outward, moon-white,
leaving no trace in the air,
and began its drop to the shore.

$$*$$

I feed upon it still, as you see;
there is no end to that which, not understood,
may yet be hoarded in the imagination,
in the yolk of one's being, so to speak,
there to undergo its (quite animal) growth,

dividing blindly, twitching, packed with will,
searching in its own tissue
for the structure in which it may wake.
Something that had – clenched in its cave –
not been now was: an egg of being.

Through what seemed a whole year it fell
– as it still falls, for me, solid and light,
the red gold beating in its silvery womb,
alive as the yolk and white of my eye.
As it will continue to fall, probably, until I die,
through the vast indifferent spaces
with which I am empty.

                              *

It smashed against the grating
and slipped down quickly out of sight.
It was over in a comical flash.
The soft mucous shell clung a little longer,
then drained down.

She stood staring, in blank anger.
Then her eyes came to life, and she laughed
and let the bird flap away.

                              'It's all the one.
There's plenty more where that came from!'

A scene ridiculous in its content, but of a serious early awareness of self and of process: of details insisting on their survival, regardless of any immediate significance.

There was another permanent finding in the same whitewashed yard, of different but not lesser importance: of selfless kindness – a first draft of love. An elderly neighbour lived in one of the cottages with his delicate and very pious wife. Born in the West of Ireland, a native speaker of Irish, he had come to Dublin and found work in the Great Southern Railway. He seemed to be always there: a friend of the family, a protector of my unformed feelings. I would visit him and his wife – leaving the shop and crossing the yard. And he would visit us in our house in Inchicore, coming across from the Railway works; doing nothing, filling some kind of lack. He died years later, in the Union in James's Street. I wrote two poems for him, in memory of his importance during those early years. Neither of the poems achieved completeness, but their parts came together:

Dick King

In your ghost, Dick King, in your phantom vowels I read
That death roves our memories igniting
Love. Kind plague, low voice in a stubbled throat,
You haunt with the taint of age and of vanished good,
Fouling my thought with losses.

Clearly now I remember rain on the cobbles,
Ripples in the iron trough, and the horses' dipped
Faces under the Fountain in James's Street,
When I sheltered my nine years against your buttons
And your own dread years were to come:

And your voice, in a pause of softness, named the dead,
Hushed as though the city had died by fire,
Bemused, discovering...discovering
A gate to enter temperate ghosthood by;
And I squeezed your fingers till you found again
My hand hidden in yours.

      I squeeze your fingers:

      Dick King was an upright man.
      Sixty years he trod
      The dull stations underfoot.
      Fifteen he lies with God.

      By the salt seaboard he grew up
      But left its rock and rain
      To bring a dying language east
      And dwell in Basin Lane.

      By the Southern Railway he increased:
      His second soul was born
      In the clangour of the iron sheds,
      The hush of the late horn.

An invalid he took to wife.
She prayed her life away;
Her whisper filled the whitewashed yard
Until her dying day.

And season in, season out,
He made his wintry bed.
He took the path to the turnstile
Morning and night till he was dead.

He clasped his hands in a Union ward
To hear St James's bell.
I searched his eyes though I was young,
The last to wish him well.

Down Bow Lane, across James's Street and nearer the river, I was making my discoveries on the Kinsella side of the family:

Bow Lane

I poked in at the back corner
of the wardrobe, at the blind
standing rolled up. It rustled
like a bat trapped inside.

There was light still coming in
over Corcorans' wall
up to the Blessed Virgin on the shelf
over the grandparents' bed.

They kept Uncle Tom's painting
hanging in there, in a black frame
– a steamer with three funnels,
and TK painted on the foam.

He died in here in 1916
of cancer of the colon. My father heard him
whispering to himself: 'Jesus,
Jesus, let me off.' But nothing worked.

I took the grey animal book
from under the clothes in the drawer
and opened it at the Capuchin monkeys
in their forest home.

I asked Tom Ryan once: 'Tell me the print!'
but he only grinned and said
'I will if you can spell Wednesday.'
With his slithery walk.

They were lighting the lamps
outside in the shop and she started shouting:
'What are you up to in there?
Always stuck in that old room.'

The grandmother Kinsella had her own hard features and qualities:

Ancestor

I was going up to say something,
and stopped. Her profile against the curtains
was old, and dark like a hunting bird's.

It was the way she perched on the high stool,
staring into herself, with one fist
gripping the side of the barrier around her desk
– or her head held by something, from inside.
And not caring for anything around her
or anyone there by the shelves.
I caught a faint smell, musky and queer.

I may have made some sound – she stopped rocking
and pressed her fist in her lap; then she stood up
and shut down the lid of the desk, and turned the key.
She shoved a small bottle under her aprons
and came toward me, darkening the passageway.

Ancestor... among sweet- and fruit-boxes.
Her black heart...
                    Was that a sigh?
– brushing by me in the shadows,
with her heaped aprons, through the red hangings
to the scullery, and down to the back room.

A particular detail, like the Baby Power whiskey bottle, would be hard for a very young observer to grasp fully; but hard to forget. Especially when it became clear, after one of the grandmother's journeys down into the back bedroom, that it was to be her last, and the bed her death-bed:

Tear

I was sent in to see her.
A fringe of jet drops
chattered at my ear
as I went in through the hangings.

I was swallowed in chambery dusk.
My heart shrank
at the smell of disused
organs and sour kidney.

The black aprons I used to
bury my face in
were folded at the foot of the bed
in the last watery light from the window

(Go in and say goodbye to her)
and I was carried off
to unfathomable depths.
I turned to look at her.

She stared at the ceiling
and puffed her cheek, distracted,
propped high in the bed
resting for the next attack.

The covers were gathered close
up to her mouth,
that the lines of ill-temper still
marked. Her grey hair

was loosened out like a young woman's
all over the pillow,
mixed with the shadows
criss-crossing her forehead

and at her mouth and eyes,
like a web of strands tying down her head
and tangling down toward the shadow
eating away the floor at my feet.

I couldn't stir at first, nor wished to,
for fear she might turn and tempt me
(my own father's mother)
with open mouth

– with some fierce wheedling whisper –
to hide myself one last time
against her, and bury my
self in her drying mud.

The details absorb in their own order. It was later in life, when I was on equal terms with my father, that something else important out of that early time became clear: the dignity and quiet of his own father, remembered as we talked about him.

With an awareness of the generations as they succeed each other. That process, with the accompanying awareness, recorded and understood, are a vital element in life as I see it now.

This is how it began:

His Father's Hands

I drank firmly
and set the glass down between us firmly.
You were saying.

My father
Was saying.

His finger prodded and prodded,
marring his point. Emphas-
emphasemphasis.

I have watched
his father's hands before him

       cupped, and tightening the black Plug
between knife and thumb,
carving off little curlicues
to rub them in the dark of his palms,

or cutting into new leather at his bench,
levering a groove open with his thumb,
insinuating wet sprigs for the hammer.

He kept the sprigs in mouthfuls
and brought them out in silvery
units between his lips.

I took a pinch out of their hole
and knocked them one by one into the wood,
bright points among hundreds gone black,
other children's – cousins and others, grown up.

       Or his bow hand scarcely moving,
scraping in the dark coner near the fire,
his plump fingers shifting on the strings

To his deaf, inclined head
he hugged the fiddle's body
whispering with the tune

with breaking heart
whene'er I hear
in privacy, across a blocked void,

the wind that shakes the barley.
The wind…
round her grave…

on my breast in blood she died…
But blood for blood without remorse
I've ta'en…

Beyond that.

                    *

Your family, Thomas, met with and helped
many of the Croppies in hiding from the Yeos
or on their way home after the defeat
in south Wexford. They sheltered the Laceys
who were later hanged on the Bridge in Ballinglen
between Tinahely and Anacorra.

From hearsay, as far as I can tell
the Men Folk were either Stone Cutters
or masons or probably both.

                         In the 18
and late 1700s even the farmers
had some other trade to make a living.

1

The History of The Kinsella or Kinchella Family. From hearsay, as far as I can tell the men folk were either Stone Cutters or masons or probably both. in the 17 and late 1800. even the Farmers had some other trade to make a living, The Kinsellas lived in Farnese; among a Colony of North of Ireland or Scotch, settlers. left there in some of the dispersals, or migrations which occurred in this Area of Wicklow Wexford & Carlow. even after the 98 Rebellion of which this part was a centre, between two big Battles, Hacketstown & Ballyraham The Kinsellas were working during that time & with the Morris Family who owned from Hacketstown to Tinahely or were Landlords of it under Coollattin. or Earl Fitzwilliam. The Kinsellas met with and helped many of the Croppies in hiding from the Yeos or on their way home after the defeat in south Wexford. And some Years before that time the Family came from somewhere round Tullow

And now comes in a family named Payne. originally living in Ballincarrig near Carlow Town. One branch lived in Croes where Hammons live now. I b- let by the Morris Family. with they were intermarried A girl of the Ballincarrig Paynes had which a Baby for some man whom She married some years after. to - how long after we can only judge by what events after. the Babe a girl was reared up near Tinahely to the house still standing. She grew up fell in love with Your Great & my Grandfather. turned Catholic & married him

They lived in Farnese among a Colony
of North of Ireland or Scotch settlers left there
in some of the dispersals or migrations
which occurred in this Area of Wicklow and Wexford
and Carlow. And some years before that time
the Family came from somewhere around Tullow.

Beyond that.

                    *

Littered uplands. Dense grass. Rocks everywhere,
wet underneath, retaining memory of the long cold.

First, a prow of land
chosen, and wedged with tracks;
then boulders chosen
and sloped together, stabilized in menace.

I do not like this place.
I do not think the people who lived here
were ever happy. It feels evil.
Terrible things happened.
I feel afraid here when I am on my own.

                    *

Dispersals or migrations.
Through what evolutions or accidents
toward that peace and patience
by the fireside, that blocked gentleness...

That serene pause, with the slashing knife,
in kindly mockery,
as I busy myself with my little nails
at the rude block, his bench.

The blood advancing
– gorging vessel after vessel –
and altering in them
one by one.

Behold, that gentleness already
modulated twice, in others:
to earnestness and iteration;
to an offhandedness, repressing various impulses.

                    *

Extraordinary… The big block – I found it
years afterward in a corner of the yard
in sunlight after rain
and stood it up, wet and black:
it turned under my hands, an axis
of light flashing down its length,
and the wood's soft flesh broke open,
countless little nails
squirming and dropping out of it.

The Messenger

In memory of John Paul Kinsella
(died May 1976)

For days I have wakened and felt immediately
half sick at something. Hour follows hour
but my shoulders are chilled with expectation.

It is more than mere loss
                              (your tomb-image
drips and blackens, my leaden root
curled on your lap)
                              or 'what you missed'.
(The hand conceives an impossible Possible
and exhausts in mid-reach.
What could be more natural?)

Deeper. A suspicion in the bones
as though they too could melt in filth.

Something to discourage goodness.

A moist movement within.
A worm winds on its hoard.
A dead egg glimmers – a pearl in muck
glimpsed only as the muck settles.

1

His mother's image settled on him
out of the dark, at the last,
and the Self sagged, unmanned.

Corded into a thick dressing gown
he glared from his rocker
at people whispering on television.

He knocked the last drops of Baby Power
into his glass and carried the lifewater
to his lips. He recollected himself

and went on with the story out of Guinness's
– the Brewery pension 'abated' by 'an amount
equal to the amount' of some pittance

on some Godforsaken pretext.
His last battle – the impulse
at its tottering extreme:

muster your fellow pensioners, and advance
pitched with them
                       ('Power to the Spent!')

against the far off boardroom door.
All about him, open mouthed,
they expired in ones and twos.

Somebody well dressed
pressed my hand in the graveyard.
A thoughtful delegated word or two:

'His father before him… Ah, the barge captain…
A valued connection. He will be well remembered…
He lived in his two sons.'

– In his own half fierce force he lived!
And stuck the first brand shakily
under that good family firm;

formed their first Union; and entered their lists.
Mason and Knight gave ground in twostep,
manager and priest disappeared

and reappeared under each other's hats;
in jigtime, to the ever popular
Faith Of Our Fathers, he was high and dry.

And in time was well remembered.
Thumbs in belt, back and forth
in stiff boots he rocked with the news

Forwarding Department.

St. James's Gate Brewery,

DUBLIN, 7th October 1901

Memorandum.

To W.P.Montgomery.Esq

F 9/2452

John Kinsella Reg No 4302

A child of the above named man having died, I beg to recommend that he shall be granted a loan of £3 for burial expenses, to be repaid at the rate of 3/- per week.

Memorandum.

ST. JAMES'S GATE BREWERY,

DUBLIN, 29th June, 19 25.

REGISTRY DEPARTMENT.

D: 4553   UJN

To

W. B. DOBBS ESQ.

John Kinsella, Reg. No.15965.

With reference to Board instruction of the 25th November 1921, that, in future, lads reaching the age of 21 are to be discharged until further notice owing to slackness of work; please note that the above-named lad was 21 years of age on the 28th instant, and he should be discharged on the 4th July, and given one week's wages in lieu of notice.

Please instruct him to call here on that day for his Reserved Wages, and his Health and Unemployment Cards.

in front of the fireplace, in his frieze jacket,
with a couple of bottles of Export in the pockets.
Florid and with scorn he stomached it

in full vigour, in his fiftieth year,
every ounce of youth
absorbed into his body.

For there is really nothing to be done.
There is an urge, and it is valuable,
but it is of no avail.

He brandished his solid body
thirty feet high above their heads therefore
and with a shout of laughter

traversed a steel beam in the Racking Shed
and dared with outstretched arms
what might befall.

And it befell that summer,
after the experimental doses,
that his bronchi wrecked him with coughs

and the muffled inner
heartstopping little
hammerblows began.

*

A brave leap   On bright prospects
in full heart   sable: a slammed
into full stop.   door.

          Vaunt and check.
          Cursus inter-
          ruptus.

Typically, there is a turning away.
The Self is islanded in fog.
It is meagre and plagued with wants

but secure. Every positive matter
that might endanger – but also enrich –
is banished. The banished matter

(a cyst, in effect, of the subject's aspirations
painful with his many disappointments)
absorbs into the psyche, where it sleeps.

Intermittently, when disturbed, it wakes
as a guardian – or 'patron' – monster
with characteristic conflicting emotional claims:

appalling, appealing; exacting sympathy
even as it threatens. (Our verb 'to haunt'
preserves the ambiguity exactly.)

A dragon slashes its lizard wings
as it looks out, with halved head,
and bellows with incompleteness.

          *

Received from Thomas Hinds the
Sum of one pound and half a years rent
due me the 25th day of March 1885 out
of his holding (part of) the Lands of
Cross Dated this 6th day of May 1885

£1 . 0 . 0   Andrew Morris

Received from Thomas Kinsella
the Sum of one pound half a years
rent due me the 29th day of September
1888 out part of the Lands of Cross.
Dated this 29 September 1888

£1 . 0 . 0   Kate Morris

It probable was a runaway marriage or Elopement. Then the Trouble started the Kinsellas were evicted by the Coolattin estate, from their Farm in Farnese. The Family dispersed. Except Thomas Kinsella and his Wife. who were allowed into the Herds Cabin down the Bog. This woman Née Payne would be either a first or Second Cousin. of Andrew Morris then living in Cross. The Family having come down in the world, due to high living and losses. He'd dug out the end of a Rath, to Build a new house in Cross. and. the Belief) of the people round here of the meddling with the Rath finished the Family, He died a bro ken hearted man, and looken in property, up to the neck in debt. (a few minor details here if interested)

Well, Grandfather & Grandmother, lived in poverty. having 3 Boys & 3 Girls Jack Mike & Thomas Kate Elizabeth & Anne. there may have been others to. Some time after Grandmother. coming to live down the Bog. Her Father and Mother Wrote. Andrew Morris as to the whereabouts of their Daughter another black mark against Morris He told them She was with him and Well I Hope. incidentally Grandfather believed he often saw and met the Ghost of Andrew Morris' long after his death.

His Widow. married Matthew Hannon Redbog. who had a bit of money. being swag in some business or other. Family there'd one Son Walties Father. Hannon

and then again we become entangled in the Payne Morris

Often, much too familiar for comfort,
the beast was suddenly there
insinuating between us:

'Who'd like to know what *I* know?'
'Who has a skeleton in *his* meat cupboard?'

'Who is inclined to lapse and let
the bone go with the dog?'

'Who flings off in a huff
and never counts the cost
as long as there's a bitter phrase
to roll around on the tongue?'

'When Guess Who polished his pointy shoe
and brushed his brilliantine
to whose admiring gaze
guess who hoodwinked Who?'

Or it would sigh and say:
'Guess who'd love to gobble *you* up!'
Or 'Who'd like to see what *I* have?'

*

I would. And have followed
the pewtery heave of hindquarters
into the fog, the wings down at heel,

until back there in the dark
the whole thing
fell on its face.

And blackened… And began
melting its details and dripping them away
little by little to reveal

him (supine, jut jawed and
incommunicable, privately
surrendering his tissues and traps).

And have watched my hand reach in under
after something, and felt it
close upon it and ease him of it.

The eggseed Goodness
that is also called
Decency.

2

Goodness is where you find it.
Abnormal.

      A pearl.

A milkblue
blind orb

      Look in it:

It is outside the Black Lion, in Inchicore.
A young man. He is not much more than thirty.
He is on an election lorry, trying to shout.

He is goodlooking and dark.
He has a raincoat belted tight
and his hair is brushed back, like what actor.

He is shouting about the Blueshirts
but his voice is hoarse.
His arm keeps pointing upward.

I am there. A dark little
blackvelvet-eyed jew-child
with leaflets.

A big Dublin face
leans down with a moustache, growling
it is a scandal.

      *

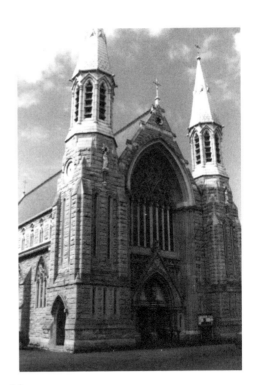

The Oblate Fathers was packed.
I sat squeezed against a cold pillar.
A bull-voice rang among the arches.

I made faces at my ghost in the brawn marble.
The round shaft went up shining
into a mouth of stone flowers

and the angry words echoed
among the hanging lamps,
off the dark golden walls.

He covered my hand with his
and we started getting out
in the middle of Mass past everybody.

Father Collier's top half in the pulpit
in a muscular black soutane and white lace
grabbed the crimson velvet ledge

– thick white hair, a red face,
a black mouth shouting
Godless Russia after us.

*

It is an August evening, in Wicklow.
It is getting late. They have tussled in love.
They are hidden, near the river bank.

They lie face up in the grass, not touching,
head close to head, a woman and her secret husband.
A gossamer ghost arrows and hesitates

out of the reeds, and stands in the air above them
insect-shimmering, and settles on a bright
inner upturn of her dress. The wings

close up like palms. The body, a glass worm,
is pulsing. The tail-tip winces and quivers:

I *think* this is where I come in.

It is! It is! Hurry!
says the great womb-whisper.
Quick! I am all egg!

                    *

Inside, it is bare but dimly alive.
Such light as there is comes in overcast
through a grey lace curtain across the window,

diffuses in the dust above the bench
and shows him stooped over his last
in a cobbler's shop. He is almost still a boy:

his hands are awkwardly readying something,
his face and shoulders are soft-handsome,
pale silver, ill at ease in the odour-bearing light.

The rest is obscure, swallowed back
in man-smells of leather and oily metal
and the faintest musk.

Beside him, his father's leaden skull
is inclined, gentle and deaf,
above the work on his apron.

The old lion-shoulders expand in the Guinness jersey,
the jaws work in his cheeks
as the quivering awl

pierces the last hole in a sole with a grunt.
He wheezes and pulls it out, and straightens.
The tide is rising and the river runs fast

into the middle span of the last bridge.
He touches the funnel on a nerve at the base
and doffs it on its hinge at the last instant

– the smoke occluding – and hauls it up again
gleaming and pluming in open water.
Here and there along the Liffey wall

he is acclaimed in friendly mockery,
humbly, saturninely, returned.
He reaches for needle and thread

patiently, as his son
struggles at the blank iron foot
in his father's den.

He will not stick at this… The knife-blades,
the hammers and pincers, the rasps and punches,
the sprigs in their wooden pits,

49

catching the light on the plank bench
among uppers and tongues and leather scraps
and black stumps of heelball.

He reaches for a hammer,
his jaw jutting as best it can
 with Marx, Engels, Larkin

howling with upstretched arms into the teeth
of Martin Murphy and the Church
and a flourish of police batons,

Connolly strapped in a chair
regarding the guns
that shall pronounce his name for ever.

Baton struck,
                gun spat,
and Martin Murphy shall change his hat.

Son and father, upright, right arms raised.
Stretching a thread.
Trying to strike right.

                    *

Deeper. The room where they all lived
behind the shop. It is dark here too – shut off
by the narrow yard. But it doesn't matter:

it is bursting with pleasure.
A new messenger boy
stands there in uniform, with shining belt!

He is all excitement: arms akimbo,
a thumb crooked by the telegram pouch,
shoes polished, and a way to make in the world.

His eyes are bright,
his schoolmaster's tags fresh in mind.
He has a few of the Gentlemen's Sixpenny Library

under the bed – *A Midsummer Night's Dream*,
Sartor Resartus, *The Divine Comedy*, with a notebook,
Moore's *Melodies*, a trifle shaken… Shelley, unbound…

He unprops the great Post Office bicycle
from the sewing machine and wheels it through the passage
by odours of apron and cabbage-water and whitewashed damp

through the shop and into the street.
It faces uphill. The urchin mounts. I see
a flash of pedals. And a clean pair of heels!

3

An eye, pale with strain, forms in the dark.
About it the iridescent
untouchable secretions collect.

It is a miracle:
the oddity nestles in slime
functionless, in all its rarity,

purifying nothing.
But nothing can befoul it,
which ought probably to console.

He rolled on rubber tyres
out of the chapel door. The oak box
paused gleaming in the May morning air

and turned, sensing its direction.
Our scattered tribe began gathering itself
and trudged off onto a gravel path after it.

By their own lightness
four girls and three boys separated themselves
out in a ragged band from our dull custom

and moved up close after it, in front,
all shapes and sizes,
grandchildren, colourful and silent.

Sometimes the memory can get a factual detail wrong, especially when it is a matter of hearsay. I knew my father began his career as a messenger; I mistook the firm...

There is another image from the same neighbourhood, later in the same time; a strange and a close one, from a phase of uncertainty and poverty. Of my father encountered for the first time as an equal; with my own growing self, over-aware, seizing on its own awareness with distinctness and déjà vu – a sign of disturbing things to come:

Irwin Street

Morning sunlight – a patch of clear memory –
warmed the path and the crumbling brick wall
and stirred the weeds sprouting in the mortar.

A sparrow cowered on a doorstep.
Under the broken door the paw of a cat
reached out.

              White nails fastened in the feathers.
Aware – a distinct dream – as though
slowly making it happen.

With my schoolbooks in my hand,
I turned the corner into the avenue
between the high wire fence and the trees in the Hospital.

Under the leaves the road was empty and fragrant
with little lances of light.
He was coming toward me, my maker,

in a white jacket, and with my face.
How could he be there, at this hour?
Our steps hesitated in awkward greeting.

        *

Wakening again upstairs.
I sat up on the edge of the bed,
my feet on the bare boards,
my hand in my pyjama trousers.

Irwin Street, like many of these places, is now only the remains of what it was: a few fragments at the end of Bow Lane, near Kingsbridge, by the Camac River.

During the 1930s we would often pass the end of it, walking on our way home from the Kinsella grandparents, crossing the small bridge over the Camac, starting on what we called the High Road, above Mount Brown, on the way to Kilmainham. This road, strangely, has managed to keep many traces of its rural past. It has no notable features. And no reason to be recorded, except for its place in the rhythm of those earliest years, insistent in the memory. And, like the grandfather Kinsella's cobbler's block, or the grandmother's apron, giving a shape of its own to what happened there:

The High Road

Don't be too long now, the next time.
She hugged me tight in behind the counter.
Here! she whispered.
                              A silvery
little mandoline, out of the sweet-box.

They were standing waiting in the sun outside
at the shop door, with the go car,
their long shadows along the path.

A horse trotted past us down Bow Lane:
Padno Carty sat in the trap
sideways, fat, drifting along
with a varnish twinkle of spokes
and redgold balls of manure scattering
behind on the road.

Mrs Fullerton was sitting on a stool
in her doorway, beak-nosed, one eye dead.
DAAARK! squawked the sour parrot in her room.
Sticking to his cage with slow nails, upside down;
creeping stiffly crossways, with his tongue
mumbling on a bar, a black moveable nut.

Silvery tiny strings
trembled in my brain.

Over the parapet of the bridge
at the end of Granny and Granda's
the brown water bubbled and poured
over the stones and tin cans in the Camac,
down by the back of Aunty Josie's.

After the bridge, a stony darkness
trickled down Cromwell's Quarters step by step,
along the foot of the wall from James's Street.
Through a barred window on one of the steps
a mob of shadows huddled in the Malt Stores
among the brick pillars and the dunes of grain.
Watching the pitch drain out of their wounds.

I held hands up the High Road
inside on the path, beside the feathery grass,
and looked down through the paling, pulled downward
by a queer feeling. Down there...windows
below the road. Small front gardens
getting lower and lower.

                      Over on the other side
a path slants up across the clay slope
and disappears into the Robbers' Den.
I crept up once to the big hole, full of fright,
and knelt on the clay to look inside.
It was only a hollow someone made,
with a dusty piece of man's dung, and bluebottles.

Not even in my mind
has one silvery string
picked a single sound.
And it will never.

Over the far-off back yards
the breeze gave a sigh: a sin happening.
I let go and stopped, and looked down
and let it fall into empty air
and watched it turning over with little flashes
silveryshivering with loss.

A first encounter with wanton impulse, abandonment and waste; unaccountable and uncontrollable. As unimportant-seeming for the scale of its content as the happening in 'Hen Woman' in Casserly's yard; but with the same direct contact with the unconscious.

Our walk continued by the high blank wall of Kilmainham – fort and prison; with no awareness of its richness in history. No more than of the shade of Swift, left behind us in Bow Lane and Steeven's Lane.

And past the great gate of Kilmainham facing Westward out of the city.

Toward Inchicore; 'island of berries'. Where the main road divided. To the left, toward the midlands, and Naas of the Kings. To the right, toward Chapelizod, on the River Liffey. On the angle of division, the triangular playground of the Model School, with the old chestnut trees; where once, when the weather was very satisfactory – and probably something else – our very good school-teacher, Mr. Brown, took us out into the sun and sat us down to share his pleasure:

Model School, Inchicore

Miss Carney handed us out blank paper and marla,
old plasticine with the colours
all rolled together into brown.

You started with a ball of it
and rolled it into a snake curling
around your hand, and kept rolling it
in one place until it wore down into two
with a stain on the paper.

We always tittered at each other
when we said the adding-up table in Irish
and came to her name.

*

In the second school we had Mr Browne.
He had white teeth in his brown man's face.

He stood in front of the blackboard
and chalked a white dot.

    'We are going to start
      decimals.'

    I am going to know
      everything.

   *

One day he said:
'Out into the sun!'
We settled his chair under a tree
and sat ourselves down delighted
in two rows in the greeny gold shade.

A fat bee floated around
shining amongst us
and the flickering sun
warmed our folded coats
and he said: 'History…!'

   *

When the Autumn came
and the big chestnut leaves
fell all over the playground
we piled them in heaps
between the wall and the tree trunks
and the boys ran races
jumping over the heaps
and tumbled into them shouting.

   *

I sat by myself in the shed
and watched the draught
blowing the papers
around the wheels of the bicycles.

Will God judge
       our most secret thoughts and actions?
God will judge
       our most secret thoughts and actions
and every idle word that man shall speak
he shall render an account of it
on the Day of Judgement.

             *

The taste
of ink off
the nib shrank your
mouth.

We would leave school at the end of the day and – a number of us – turn left together, running for a little while, then under the railway bridge and home, into The Ranch.

A curious settlement of four short streets sealed off by two others, one at either end. A pleasant place, at that time still in the country: the narrow road at the corner, lined with blackberry bushes, starting toward Chapelizod. Where Tristram, we were told, came for Isolde.

Chapelizod was certainly a magical-looking place on the river in the distance, as we looked toward it in the evening from the Liffey Hill in The Ranch.

The Ranch itself, though it was a considerable distance from anywhere, was a practical place, with a shop and its own pub and a great neighbourliness. I have always believed – though I have not checked this – that it was built for workers in the Great Southern Railway. The Railway works were there opposite, across an empty stretch of land, and reached by a walled-in passageway, through a turnstile directly facing St. Mary's Terrace. This passageway led nowhere but into the works, and was called the Khyber Pass. And here is where Dick King emerged when he came to visit us in our house on Phoenix Street.

Phoenix Street... It seemed an imaginative name. But the next street was Park Street. And I can see the planner idling over his map, looking Northward from his site across the Liffey, at the Phoenix Park. And settling for the first two titles to hand...

Beside the Liffey, looking across at the Fifteen Acres in the Park, I spent the best part of my own beginning. And, in Number 37 Phoenix Street, made my first encounter as an infant with people outside the family, our good and friendly neighbours. Staring at the stranger; at the other – across the dividing wall – into Number 38:

38 Phoenix Street

Look.
       I was lifted up
past rotten bricks weeds
to look over the wall.
A mammy lifted up a baby on the other side.
Dusty smells. Cat. Flower bells
hanging down purple red.

Look.
       The other. Looking.
My finger picked at a bit of dirt
on top of the wall and a quick
wiry redgolden thing
ran back down a little hole.

       *

We knelt up on our chairs in the lamplight
and leaned on the brown plush, watching the gramophone.
The turning record shone and hissed
under the needle, liftfalling, liftfalling.
John McCormack chattered in his box.

Two little tongues of flame burned
in the lamp chimney, wavering
their tips. On the glass belly
little drawnout images quivered.
Jimmy's mammy was drying the delph in the shadows.

       *

Mister Cummins always hunched down
sad and still beside the stove,
with his face turned away toward the bars.
His mouth so calm, and always set so sadly.
A black rubbery scar stuck on his white forehead.

Sealed in his sad cave. Hisshorror erecting
slowly out of its rock nests, nosing the air.
He was buried for three days under a hill of dead,
the faces congested down all round him
grinning *Dardanelles*! in the dark.

They noticed him by a thread of blood
glistening among the black crusts on his forehead.
His heart gathered all its weakness, to beat.

A worm hanging down, its little round
black mouth open. Sad father.

                    *

I spent the night there once
in a strange room, tucked in against the wallpaper
on the other side of our own bedroom wall.

Up in the corner of the darkness the Sacred Heart
leaned down in his long clothes over a red oil lamp
with his women's black hair and his eyes lit up in red,
hurt and blaming. He held out the Heart
with his women's fingers, like a toy.

The lamp-wick, with a tiny head
of red fire, wriggled in its pool.
The shadows flickered: the Heart beat!

When I was growing up, a great deal of Dublin outside of these two small districts would have seemed threatening and strange. And all of these poems, whatever their differences, have a feature in common: a tendency to look inward for material – into family or self. When a number of individual books were collected and published later, the collection was called *Blood and Family*.

But it is hard to keep the world out forever. And the beginning, frightening and necessary, in our next-door-neighbour's bedroom, was succeeded through various stages. In the late 1930s – shortly after the outbreak of war – my father, ill-advised, decided to move us from the seclusion of The Ranch to Manchester: I believe in pursuit of steady work. I remember the air raid sirens and the searchlights; being taken down into the shelters, and the sound and the reverberations of the explosions overhead.

It was a short episode. Our family returned to Dublin, and to a different uneasy world: of displacement and unemployment, and short stays in strange houses – one of them in Irwin Street... With a brief return to the Model School; then being passed on to the Christian Brothers, in O'Connell School on the North side, for my secondary education. And of re-settlement: our finding a tiny house in Basin Lane – a few doors from the Casserly shop; cycling to school and meeting the new teachers – a succession of Christian Brothers and lay teachers, varying in their ability as teachers and varying greatly in character: one strict to the point of cruelty, unforgettable; another gentle – gentlemanly – efficient and understanding, unforgettable also. And studying there through the remaining years of the war, getting to know Dublin for myself.

I finished secondary school in 1946 and moved, after the summer, with a scholarship, and great excitement, to UCD, looking forward to a career in science; until, on a day in winter, in a laboratory in the University – watching certain solvents reacting in their glass phials – I realised I could not devote my future to this work.

A friend I had left school with had done an examination, for entry into the Civil Service; I had done it with him, at his suggestion, and partly to keep him company. About the time of my lost faith in science, I received a letter saying I had succeeded in the Civil Service examination, and that there was work available if I wanted it, permanent and pensionable.

By the end of the year I was a junior executive officer in the Irish Land Commission, dealing with the affairs of the old Congested Districts Board. And fascinated. By the array of my colleagues; but above all by the work. This was living history, daily activities based still in the country's past: acquisition of the old landlord estates, and their subdivision and resale among the resident tenants – the dispossessed. Great work was done by the Land Commission inspectors on the ground; their reports an important archive, compassionate and understanding. A few years into this period, I was told of another examination: for a different, and higher, grade in the Service. I did this, and found myself once more among the successful. I transferred to the Department of Finance, with an office in Government Buildings on Merrion Street, sharing corridors with very senior figures entering and leaving their offices, and with Ministers and Heads of State at their Government meetings. And participating in the workings of Government: at the junction of politics and administration. On the political front, drafting answers to Parliamentary questions, or preparing details for the national annual Budget. On the administrative, co-ordinating the work of other – and specialist – Departments; dealing with occasional difficult, or marginal, individual problems.

All of this in a brief, high-seasoned bachelorhood. Moving out of home and onto a new base: in a dark and unhealthy single room, under the roof of an old house on Baggot Street – around the corner from the Department; and in walking distance of everything of interest in the city. Including a meetingplace with a number of students of literature.

I had discovered, somehow, the poetry of W. H. Auden and been struck by its emotional and technical relevance for myself. Poetry, for the first time, was a meaningful human activity. Our dealings with poetry in school had been meaningless: a mechanical and unfeeling manipulation of mainly Romantic verse, organising our responses totally toward the answering of possible examination questions. Now I was electrified, by the life and relevance in Auden's work – and by the realisation that the medium of poetry, in this living manifestation, was of importance to myself.

This, at last, was the matter of interest. And in the peace and relative squalor of my single room, looking South over the city roofs toward the Dublin mountains, I made my first serious attempt at writing verse.

From very early in this latter process – dealing with it live, as it happened:

Baggot Street Deserta

Lulled, at silence, the spent attack.
The will to work is laid aside.
The breaking-cry, the strain of the rack,
Yield, are at peace. The window is wide
On a crawling arch of stars, and the night
Reacts faintly to the mathematic
Passion of a cello suite
Plotting the quiet of my attic.

A mile away the river toils
Its buttressed fathoms out to sea;
Tucked in the mountains, many miles
Away from its roaring outcome, a shy
Gasp of waters in the gorse
Is sonneting origins. Dreamers' heads
Lie mesmerised in Dublin's beds
Flashing with images, Adam's morse.

A cigarette, the moon, a sigh
Of educated boredom, greet
A curlew's lingering threadbare cry
Of common loss. Compassionate,
I add my call of exile, half-
Buried longing, half-serious
Anger and the rueful laugh.
We fly into our risk, the spurious.

Versing, like an exile, makes
A virtuoso of the heart,
Interpreting the old mistakes
And discords in a work of Art
For the One, a private masterpiece
Of doctored recollections. Truth
Concedes, before the dew, its place
In the spray of dried forgettings Youth
Collected when they were a single
Furious undissected bloom.
A voice clarifies when the tingle
Dies out of the nerves of time:
Endure and let the present punish.
Looking backward, all is lost;
The Past becomes a fairy bog
Alive with fancies, double crossed
By pad of owl and hoot of dog,
Where shaven, serious-minded men
Appear with lucid theses, after
Which they don the mists again
With trackless, cotton-silly laughter;
Secretly a swollen Burke
Assists a decomposing Hare
To cart a body of good work
With midnight mutterings off somewhere;
The goddess who had light for thighs
Grows feet of dung and takes to bed,
Affronting horror-stricken eyes,
The marsh bird that children dread.

I nonetheless inflict, endure,
Tedium, intracordal hurt,
The sting of memory's quick, the drear
Uprooting, burying, prising apart
Of loves a strident adolescent
Spent in doubt and vanity.
All feed a single stream, impassioned
Now with obsessed honesty,
A tugging scruple that can keep
Clear eyes staring down the mile,
The thousand fathoms, into sleep.

Fingers cold against the sill
Feel, below the stress of flight,
The slow implosion of my pulse
In a wrist with poet's cramp, a tight
Beat tapping out endless calls
Into the dark, as the alien
Garrison in my own blood
Keeps constant contact with the main
Mystery, not to be understood.
Out where imagination arches
Chilly points of light transact
The business of the border-marches
Of the Real, and I – a fact
That may be countered or may not –
Find their privacy complete.

My quarter-inch of cigarette
Goes flaring down to Baggot Street.

And once, in that room, at a turning point in a complicated and continuing love story, I heard a knock on the door:

The Familiar

I

I was on my own, fumbling at the neglect
in my cell, up under the roof
over Baggot Street. Remembering
our last furious farewell
– face to face, studying each other
with a hardness like hate.
Mismatched, under the sign of sickness.

My last thoughts alone.
Her knock at the door:
her face bold on the landing.
'I brought you a present.'

I lifted in her case.
It was light, but I could tell
she was going to stay.

II

The demons over the door
        that had watched over me
        and my solitary shortcomings

looked down upon us
        entering together
        with our animal thoughts

III

Muse on my mattress
       with eyes bare
combing her fingers
       down through my hair

Her things on the floor
       a sigh of disorder
box of her body
       in an oxtail odour

Bending above me
       with busy neck
and loose locks
       my mind black

But that is the beginning of a different range of affairs: of family life in the Southern suburb of Sandycove; of years of service in the Department of Finance; and of a growing – and conflicting – commitment to poetry.

part II:
… second roots …

In 1965 I resigned from the Department and took up a different career closer to my main interest, in two Universities in the United States, with small classes and the close reading of poems.

I soon discovered there was another need – a serious academic American interest in the Irish tradition – that I could satisfy in Ireland, with the help of certain acquaintances and friends very expert in the various fields: of archaeology, geography and history, folk studies and the literature in both languages. We established a study programme in Dublin, and our family returned, to spend most of each year in the city.

We found a pleasant house in the city centre, on Percy Place beside Huband Bridge, across the Canal from the Peppercanister Church, within sound of the church bell on Haddington Road, and with a coalman and his horse in our mews on Percy Lane.

We made ourselves quickly at home, and set down our second roots in Dublin.

78

The Stable

A loft, out of the market place,
of beams and whitened stone. Where the feed
was forked out, down to the Lane.

The ivy opposite, crept at last
over the date and initials painted
big and uneasy on the wall.
Where he kept the dray, half stacked with sacks.

O'Keeffe.
          Unbothered for forty years
he took the path from the stable door
to the garden tap, and ran the water
into the bucket under his thumb.
He held the rim up spilling against
the teeth and the rubber lips of the horse
shifting its hooves in the wheaten stink

Starting out, at the cross lane,
it smelled the water off the Canal,
and fidgeted with a creak of straps
– tossing its face and rearing back
in the black tackle, half in earnest.
Then settled down between the shafts.

When O'Keeffe got sick
the wife and the helpful son-in-law
manoeuvred it out for the last time.
She waited back in the stable, crying.
They both knew well the kind of hold
they were handing over with the key.

When O'Keeffe came out his every move
was new and deliberate, exercising
along the Canal as far as the Lane
and back again by Haddington Road.

We sat in the kitchen across from each other:
I said Three Pounds. He made it Five.
We shook hands and I wrote it down
– the cash to be left on the window sill
where he left the rent.

And he wasn't gone
a month when the local roughs were in.

The Bell

The bell on Haddington Road rang,
a fumbled clang behind the flats.
Anderson calling to his neighbour.

Hauling down on the high rope,
announcing his iron absolutes
audible in Inchicore.

Disturbing the sanctuary lamp
– cup of blood, seed of light,
hanging down from their dark height.

The Back Lane

The long workroom, in a dead light
        and brain and book odour, as it was left.
The book I came for was still open

at the title-page and the sharp
        elderly down-tasting profile.
Close it with one finger, and gather it up.

                *

Outside, in the first night air,
        the double timber door scraped across
shut, under the wet vine.

I leaned back against the wood
        on serpent terms with Comers' cat
on the wall opposite, deadly in the open.

A black stain of new tar on the ground
        – shade that in the beginning
moved on the concrete.

And the remains of a cement mash
        emptied direct on the clay; betraying
the carelessness of the telephone people,

the slovenliness of the City and its lesser works.
        Culpable ignorance, distinguishing Man
from the cat and the other animals.

I stirred a half brain of cauliflower
        with my foot, on wet paper
against the corrugated tin and the neglect next door.

The Moon had set.
        And the Plough, emblem of toil.
And my own sign had descended.

Three Corporation lamps lit the way
        along the wall to the far corner,
and I started down the middle of the Lane

with the book at my heart
        and the pen patted in its pocket.
Past stables and back gates

in various use and ruin:
        vegetable and mongrel smells, a scent of clay
and roots and spinster flesh.

                    *

It was something to do with this
        brought me looking for you at this hour.
Not anything to do with management or method

– prejudice veiled as justice, the particulars
        rearranged with a mathematical scowl;
or your childlike direct way with system.

But the smell of exit:

>the next,

>>and last, excitement.

With a simple form imposed

>– these three lamps brightening and embracing
and fading behind me in the dark.

As far as the cross lane,

>and out among your larger works, City Fathers,
into the world of waste.

>>*

I stopped at the junction

>in a first smell of water off the Canal,
and allowed myself a prayer, with open arms

– the right arm held up hanging empty,

>the left lifting my book;
with the wrists nailed back:

Lord, grant us a local watchfulness.

>Accept us into that minority
driven toward a totality of response,

and I will lower these arms

>and embrace what I find.
Embarrassed.

Encountering my brother figure.
      – Startled likewise, in that posture
of seeming shyness, then glaring,

lips set and dark,
      hands down and averted
that have dipped in the same dish with mine.

But it was no one I knew,
      hurrying out onto the terrace,
the features withdrawn and set in shame.

The Stranger

Years ago, while we were settling in,
I saw him passing by this side of the Canal,
a clerk from somewhere in the area.

Then, more accustomed to the neighbourhood,
I noticed him the other side of the Bridge,
crossing over from Mount Street opposite

or turning away in the dark along the base
of the heavy-set terrace, back around the Church
with the little peppercanister cupola.

One evening, when our house was full of neighbours
met in upset, I was standing by the drapes
and saw his face outside, turned up to the light.

And once in Baggot Street I was talking with someone
when he passed with a word or two to the other, his face
arab up close. We smiled in antipathy.

In another time I might have put it down
to evil luck or early death – the Stranger
close upon our heels – and taken care.

But you and I were starting to deal already
with troubles any Stranger might desire.
Our minds in their teeming patterns died each night.

Once, at an upper window, at my desk,
with the photographs and cuttings pinned in fury
around the wall, and tacked across the blind,

I found a structure for my mess of angers,
lifted out of the school dark:
                            Distracted

one morning by a stream, in circumstances
of loveliness and quiet, not for him,
a poet sinks to the ground and hides his face

in harrowed sleep. A kindly beauty approaches,
unworldly, but familiar – one of us –
comforts his misery, and turns his thoughts

toward some theatrical hope…
                            He reawakens,
distracted still.

A simple form; adjusting
simply with the situation,
and open to local application; weakened

by repetition; ridiculed and renewed
at last in parody. My pen quickened
in a pulse of doggerel ease.

When I beheld him the other side of the road,
overacting, bowing with respect;
resuming his night patrol along the terrace.

Leaving my fingers stopped above the paper.

Our new home brought a number of things and times together. It was in easy walking distance of the first flat in Baggot Street. Across the Canal, and beyond the Church, it faced down the Georgian vista of Mount Street and South Merrion Square, toward Government Buildings. The same vista, in the other direction, and ending perfectly in the Peppercanister Church, that I had seen each day as I entered and left the Department.

The Department – the site of my first off-key career; and of certain findings, in matter and method, that I have appreciated more and more for writing, as the years have passed; that have helped toward viewing things directly, staying with the relevant data, and transmitting them complete.

And once, on a disturbed evening, I left our second Dublin home and found myself walking back into the old city to find my past again: back into the neighbourhood of Thomas Street and James's Street, places of family and family friends – old places, many of them demolished or built-over, all of them changed. This time with an awareness of their riches in history, and of another disturbed figure, like Swift's in the shadows:

St Catherine's Clock

The whole terrace
slammed shut.
I inhaled the granite lamplight,
divining the energies of the prowler.

A window opposite, close up.
In a corner, a half stooped image
focused on the intimacy
of the flesh of the left arm.

The fingers of the right hand are set
in a scribal act on the skin:
a gloss, simple and swift as thought,
is planted there.

The point uplifted,
wet with understanding,
he leans his head a moment
against the glass.

              I see.

Thomas Street. At the first hour

The clock
on the squat front of St Catherine's
settled a gilded point
up soundless into place.

1803

After the engraving by George Cruikshank

Lord Kilwarden, genuflected
prim and upset outside his carriage door,
thrown back rhetorical

among a pack of hatted simians,
their snouted malice gathered
into the pike-point entering his front.

His two coachmen
picked, like his horses, from a finer breed
register extremes of shocked distress.

Somewhere a nephew,
Mr Richard Wolfe, is fallen
and spilling his share of blood and matter.

from a non-contemporary nationalist artist's impression

And Robert Emmet on the scaffold high,
as close as possible to the site of the outrage,
is dropped from his brief height

into a grove of redcoats
mounted with their rumps
toward a horrified populace.

The torch of friendship and the lamp of life
extinguished, his race finished,
the idol of his soul offered up,

sacrificed on the altar of truth and liberty,
awaiting the cold honours of the grave,
requiring only the charity of silence,

he has done.

The sentence pronounced in the usual form,

he has bowed and retired.

The pasty head is separated and brandished aloft,

the dead forehead with the black wet lock

turned toward the Fountain.

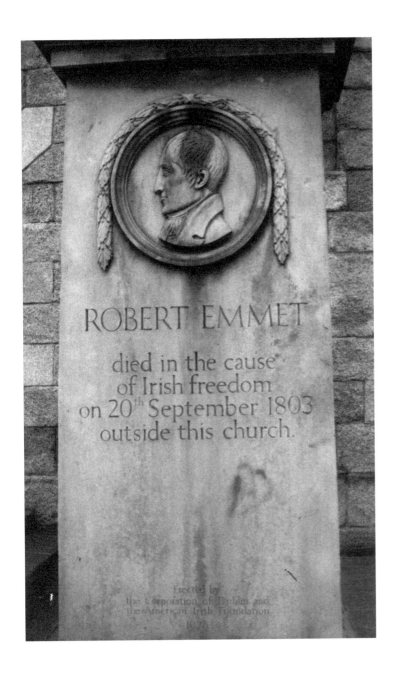

ROBERT EMMET

died in the cause
of Irish freedom
on 20th September 1803
outside this church.

Erected by
the Corporation of Dublin and
the American Irish Foundation

1792

Jas. Malton, del.

At the drink shop by the Church corner
two horsemen are greeting,
their mounts brow to brow.

In the background
some activity about the water fountain:
a pair of children or dwarfs,

a man and women with buckets,
a couple of mongrels
worrying the genitals out of each other.

Centre, barefoot,
bowed in aged rags to the earth,
a hag

toils across the street
on her battered business,
a drained backside

turned toward St Catherine;
everybody, even those
most near, turned away.

Right foreground, a shade waits for her
humped man-shaped against a dark cart
with whipstaff upright.

Set down to one side
by unconcerned fingers, a solitary redcoat
is handling the entire matter.

Past the Watch House and Watling Street
beyond St James's Gate, a pale blue
divides downhill into thin air

on a distant dream
of Bow Lane
and Basin Lane.

1938

On the dark shelf up behind her head
the silk-soft red-and-black
tin tea boxes out of India
were matched beside each other.

She was settling the round little weights
on top of each other,
                    smaller and smaller,
with her knuckles and long black nails

beside the iron weighing-scales on the counter:
the cross-beam, with the black flat flowers,
balanced; the two brass pans, equal,
hanging in their chains.

The fat sugar sack, with the twiny neck rolled back,
was kept tucked against her stool
and her high boot, laced up
under her brown skirt.

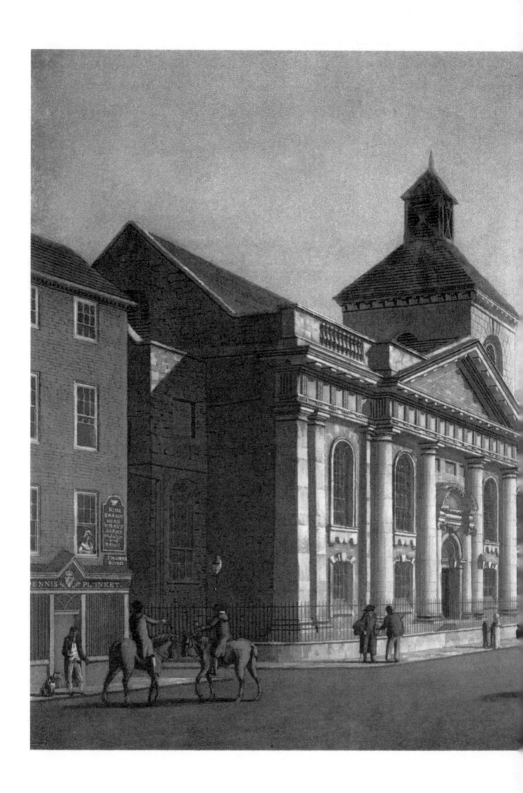

James Malton del. et fecit.

97

You could tell when the goose eggs from down the country
were in far on the low shelf
on the way down to the back;
green and grey, the fill of your palm.

I was inside in the back room
up on their bed with a rolled-up newspaper
at the holy picture, killing flies.
It gave, in a bed smell, when I moved across it.

There was one on the face of the Sacred Heart.
With its black little pointed head
and dead eyes looking everywhere.
Twining and wiping its thin paws.

But somebody in the other room
shouted my name, and it started
flying around with the others
at angles up under the light bulb.

Sometimes some of the aunts
wouldn't talk for weeks,
in a bad temper after passing remarks.

They chewed their lips
and passed each other by
with stiff faces.

But some of them would keep
muttering together in the middle room.
And one of them would suddenly

laugh up out of her throat,
and all the put-on pain and high snout
would go out of their stares.

Up the bright road starting toward Naas
with the line of new houses
going up the long hill
out into the country

we turned off into a hidden
street of brown houses
down to a door in the quiet corner
to visit our best cousins,

older, handsome boys, with good teeth,
all three of them doing well,
two of them always
understanding and good.

Out near the country
we shouted at one another everywhere

– even in whispers, out over the river bank,
holding onto the rushes, hardly breathing,

looking down through our shadows into the water
for the sign of a striped perch

pretending among the reeds, to see it move
– and drop a stone in, scattering our faces.

*

Sometimes it sounded like she was giving out
but she was really minding us.

I know I was not bold
even if I did terrible things.

I was always dressed properly,
and minded my brother.

One night we scrounged up together
and felt the little eggs in each other.

And I always remembered
who and what I am.

The balm of a clouded breast…
The musk of a stocking rolled down
over her pale knee beside the fire-place.

Then left by myself
sitting up in the fire shadows,
little fingertip touches

flickering reddened
over my picture book.
I let the book fall after a while

and an uncertain shade
started trying to get up,
with the wings dragging;

then upright in beauty,
his pinions touched with the red firelight.
He turned his golden head.

But when I woke it was all restless
with the stare of love's hatred
and you that know well and will not know

and ill-will spitting
casual at the street corner, ignorant
born and bred.

The Night crept
among our chalk signs on the path
and trickled down into the shores.

The moon hung round and silver
out over the empty Back
between the backs of the people's houses

where we piled the rubbish up
on the clay in the dark
and set it on fire and talked into the flames

and skipped around in wickedness
with no mercy on the weak or the fat
or the witless or the half blind.

                    *

I have struggled, hand
over hand,
in the savage dance.

I have lain inert, the flesh in nightmare,
eating and eaten,
with eyes wide open.

And I have sat solitary
outside, on the low window-sill,
a brutal nail nagging out of nowhere.

Grand Canal Place.
       At the second hour.
Live lights on oiled water
       in the terminus harbour.

Not fifty yards from here
she took the certificate
and slapped it down on the table.
It took that to shut them up.

Kathleen was very good
and Matty kindness itself.
With three sons of their own
they put her up for the birth.

Nurse Fitzsimons looked after her
out of the long bag. She was very fat
and looked after the whole neighbourhood
for twenty years afterwards.

His voice, empty and old,
came around to it more than once:
something about the family
he had to tell me sometime.

A dead voice now
in my ear: You can be certain
from your own cold certainties
that you are a son of hers.

But you would have to try
very far under my feeble force
to find anything more
than a passing kind of doggedness.

Closer than a brother
(born of the same woman,
face down face up to her fondness,
and a quiet brutal other

closer than a brother)
look for the dimpled smile
empty of understanding
that will tell you the rest of it.

I leave you a few faint questions
and good and bad example
and things I have not told you,
and who and what you are.

Bridie, the next and youngest,
the musical one of the family,
was hardly like an aunt at all,

bright and sharp, so unlucky
with her first love lost or dead
in Rio de Janeiro.

She knelt down quickly beside me
with her handbag and her schoolteacher's smile
for a hurried hug and goodbye,

the pair of us so alike,
everybody agreed,
wherever we got our brains.

James's Street.
                    Turning a night face
and my own thin hair feeling the wet
away from the Fountain and some that are most near.

Back past St Catherine's:
a modest bloody little trickle
spilling from the foot of the ghost scaffold

and starting down with the slope,
sensing the first possibility of a direction
– ghost handkerchiefs dipped with tears in its course;

sensing the far-off river
flowing toward freedom between high block walls;
the new soul struggling with wet wings

till it come to some more friendly port
to give it shelter against the heavy storms
with which it is buffeted.

Long lost, a second-last letter,
written in his own tears,
was found in the stuffing of a sofa.

1740

At the other end of the darkened market place
a man's figure crossed over
out of Francis Street

reading the ground,
all dressed in black
like a madwoman.

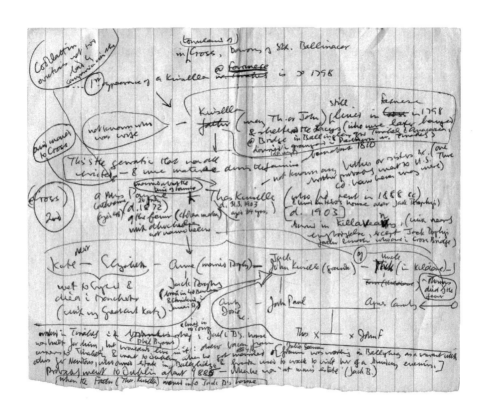

THE HISTORY OF THE KINSELLA OR KINCHELLA FAMILY

The following is a handwritten history of the family, written by Jack Brophy, an uncle of Thomas Kinsella.

From hearsay, as far as I can tell, The men Folk were either Stone Cutters or Masons or probably both. in the 17 and late 1800. even the Farmers had some other trade to make a living. The Kinsellas lived in Farnese (it's now White Rock) among a colony of North of Ireland or Scotch, settlers left there in some of the dispersals, or migrations which occurred in this Area of Wicklow, Wexford and Carlow. even after the, 98 Rebellion of which this part was a centre, between two big Battles, Hacketstown and Ballyrahan. The Kinsellas were working during that time with the Morris Family who owned from Hacketstown to Tinahely or were landlords of it under Coollattin or Earl Fitzwilliam. The Kinsellas met with and helped many of the Croppies in hiding from the Yeos or on their way home after the defeat in south Wexford. And some years before that time the Family came from somewhere round Tullow.

And now comes in a family named Payne, originally living in Ballincarrig near Carlow town. One branch lived in Cross where Hannons live now. Sub-let by the Morris Family – with which they were intermarried. A girl of the Ballincarrig Paynes had a baby for some man whom she married some years after – how long after we can only judge by events after. The baby a girl was reared up near Tinahely the house still standing. She grew up and fell in love with your Great and my Grandfather turned Catholic and married him.

It probably was a runaway marriage or Elopement. Then the Trouble started, the Kinsellas were evicted by the Coolattin estate, from their farm in Farnese. The

Family dispersed, except Thomas Kinsella and his wife, who were allowed into the Herds Cabin down the Bog. This woman Lee Payne would be either a first or Second Cousin of Andrew Morris then living in Cross. The Family having come down in the world due to high living and losses. He'd dug out the end of a Rath, to build a new house in Cross, and the belief of the people round here the meddling with the Rath finished the Family. He died a broken hearted man, and broken in property, up to his neck in debt. (a few minor details here if interested)

Well Grandfather and Grandmother lived in poverty, having 3 boys and 3 girls. Jack Mike and Thomas Kate Elizabeth & Anne. There may have been others too. Some time after Grandmother coming to live down the Bog. Her Father and Mother wrote Andrew Morris as to the whereabouts of their Daughter another black mark against Morris. He told them She was with him and Well & Happy. Incidentally Grandfather believed he often saw and met the ghost of Andrew Morris, long after his death.

His widow married Matthew Hannon Redbog who had a bit of money being away in some business or other.

They'd one son Wallie's father.

And then again we become entangled in the Payne, Morris, Hannon Family.

The Payne Family that lived in Cross got broke, emigrated to Australia and prospered there. A girl came to Cross on a Visit during my School days to look up her Morris Relations. And she was wealthy.

A bad fever raged round the country in 1871. My mother was a baby Some old woman called in to see Grandmother down the Bog. This Woman was after preparing two fever corpses for burial on the Redbog across the river. The Kinsellas got the Fever. Grandmother & Thomas dying and how the rest managed to live I never found out. My mother was reared in a Relations Family in Tinahely until she was able to look after Herself & Grandfather. They moved up here in 1880 a big privilege at the time a house with a Set Rent Two Pounds and rates to the County Council.

LIST OF ILLUSTRATIONS

ILLUSTRATIONS THAT
RELATE TO POEMS